FISHING

LISA KLOBUCHAR

Heinemann Library
Chicago, Illinois

Customer Service   888–454–2279

Visit our website at www.heinemannlibrary.com

Photo research by Jill Birschbach
Designed by Joanna Turner
Illustrations by Jeff Edwards (p. 15) and Barry Atkinson (p. 19)
Originated by Ambassador Litho Ltd.
Printed in China by WKT Company Ltd.

10 09 08
10 9 8 7 6 5 4 3 2

Library of Congress Cataloging-in-Publication Data

Klobuchar, Lisa.
  Fishing / by Lisa Klobuchar.
     p. cm. — (Get going! hobbies)
Includes bibliographical references (p.   ) and index.
  ISBN 1-4034-6117-1 (hardcover) — ISBN 1-4034-6124-4 (pbk.)
  1. Fishing—Juvenile literature. [1. Fishing.] I. Title. II. Series.
  SH445.K58 2004
  799.1—dc22

                              2003025932

Acknowledgments
The author and publisher are grateful to the following for permission to reproduce copyright material: p. 4 George Shelley/Corbis; pp. 5, 8, 9b, 12, 13, 14, 15, 16, 17, 20, 21b, 23, 24 Dale Spartas Photo; p. 6t The Art Archive/Picture Desk; p. 6b The Granger Collection, New York; p. 7 Richard Hamilton Smith; p. 9t Doug Stamm/Stammphoto; p. 11 Lawrence Manning/Corbis; p. 18 Steve Maslowski/Visuals Unlimited; p. 21t Ariel Skelley/Corbis; p. 22t Used with permission of the Illinois Department of Natural Resources; p. 22b Jeff Greenberg/Photo Edit; p. 26t Kevin Fleming/Corbis; p. 26b Hooked on Fishing International; p. 28 Dinodia; p. 29 Reuters NewMedia Inc./Corbis

Cover photograph of fishers by Dale Spartas Photo

Special thanks to Sam Detrent, an experienced fisher and hunter, for his comments that were used to complete this book.

CONTENTS

What Is Fishing? 4

Fishing History. 6

Choosing Your Rod and Reel 8

Tackling the Tackle Box 10

Choosing Your Bait 12

Setting Up Your Rig 14

Casting 16

Finding Fish. 18

Playing and Landing Fish 20

Following the Rules 22

Cooking and Eating Fish. 24

Competitions. 26

Fishing Around the World. 28

Glossary 30

More Books to Read. 31

Taking It Further 31

Index 32

Some words are shown in bold, **like this.** You can find out what they mean by looking in the glossary.

Part of the fun of fishing is the mystery. As your line disappears into the water, you try to imagine what is going on under the surface. Is your hook and bait just dangling unnoticed in deep water? Or is a hungry fish eyeing it, getting ready to snap it up?

Suddenly you feel a little tug on the line. Could this be a fish? You feel another tug. This time there is no doubt—you have a bite. Now you have to make a split-second decision. Does the fish have the hook in its mouth, or is it just testing? If you pull back on the rod too soon or too late, the fish will escape.

REELING IN YOUR CATCH

If you have some experience with fishing, you will know just what to do. With perfect timing, you jerk up the tip of your rod. The tugging on your line tells you that you have hooked your fish. Not too quickly and not too slowly, you reel in your catch.

Sometimes, you have to fight to bring in a big one!

ANGLING

The sport of fishing with a hook, line, and rod is called angling. The word comes from an old English word meaning "hook." People fish in lakes, streams, rivers, ponds, reservoirs, and oceans. In this book you will learn all about the sport of freshwater angling.

Fishing can be fun for people of all ages. This girl holds a big rainbow trout that she caught.

IS FISHING CRUEL?

For many anglers, their enjoyment of the sport depends on their belief that hooking fish does not cause the fish pain. A scientific study in the United States in 2003 also suggested that this was true. The study found that fish brains do not have the necessary regions to allow the fish to experience pain. However, another study in Great Britain seemed to show that fish do feel pain. It showed that when irritating substances were put on the skin of a fish, the fish behaved as if it was bothered. People who want to discourage others from fishing point to this new research as proof that hooking a fish through the mouth with a sharp hook is cruel.

Humans have been fishing for tens of thousands of years. **Archaeologists** have found evidence that people in southern Africa knew how to fish as early as 100,000 years ago. People back then probably speared fish to catch them. The oldest known fish hooks were found in eastern Europe. They date from about 20,000 years ago and are made of horn, bone, and wood. All over the world, archaeologists have found ancient remains of hooks, spear tips, fishnets, and weights used in fishing.

The earliest record of people fishing as a pastime is from ancient Greece. The Greek poet Theocritus, who lived in about 280 B.C.E., wrote the first known description of fishing with a pole and line. At about the same time, the Chinese were using silk line and metal hooks to pull in fish for fun.

This Egyptian artwork showing two fishers in a boat is more than 4,000 years old.

FIRST BOOK ABOUT FISHING

The first surviving full-length book on fishing for sport is *The Treatyse of Fysshynge Wyth an Angle*, published in 1496. That title in today's English would be *The Treatise of Fishing with an Angle*. Historians believe that its author was a nun named Dame Juliana Berners. She wrote that anglers should fish with a spirit of love and respect for nature in mind. She encouraged anglers to make all their own equipment and gave readers instructions on how to do it.

This drawing of a fisher was used in a book in 1496.

FISHING AS A HOBBY

The development of manufacturing in the mid-1800s gave many people an opportunity to experience angling as a hobby. New types of rods were developed, and the first reliable reel was invented. The first spinning reels became available in the early 1900s. In the 1930s and 1940s, **synthetic** lines and **fiberglass** rods were invented. Fishing equipment was improved both in variety and quality in the second half of the 1900s. New kinds of materials made rods stronger and more sensitive. Anglers today use electronic devices to determine water depth and to "see" what is under the water. Some even use satellite technology to find and mark good fishing spots.

Today, angling is more popular than ever, with more than 28 million freshwater anglers in the United States. More people fish for fun than play golf and tennis combined.

This type of fishing boat is used to fish for bass in particular.

FISH LINGO

Here are a few popular fishing expressions and their meanings:

backlash tangle of fishing line that results from a bad cast
bird's nest big mass of fishing line that is really hard to untangle
cross a fish's eyeballs to set the hook
dink small fish, especially a small bass
hammer to take the bait swiftly, suddenly, and aggressively
honey hole good fishing spot where many fish are gathered and biting
hammer handle small young northern pike, so called because it is long and thin. Also called a snake.
horse to use too much force when reeling in a fish
lunker big fish
smoke when a fish swims far and fast with the bait

The most basic fishing equipment is the rod and reel. Today's rods are made of various materials such as fiberglass and **graphite.** Some rods are long, and others are short. Some bend very easily, while others are stiff. Anglers also have several different types of reels to choose from. Anglers use different rod and reel **rigs** depending on what kind of fishing they are doing. To fish for small panfish, such as sunfish, a small reel and a short, lightweight rod that bends easily are best. **Landing** a fifteen-pound (seven-kilogram) fish usually requires a longer, stiffer rod and a sturdy reel.

The photo below shows some of the parts of fishing rods and reels.

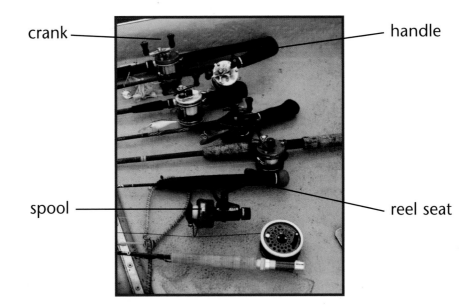

crank — handle

spool — reel seat

FOUR MAIN TYPES OF REELS

All reels have a spool for holding a line and some kind of crank for **retrieving** a **lure.** A *spincaster* is the easiest kind of reel for beginners to use. The spool that holds the line is enclosed in a case. The angler can cast easily with little chance of tangling the line.

A *spinning reel* has an open spool with a thin, metal loop called a **bail.** An angler flips the bail over to cast or to let out some line. Spinning reels are the most popular because they are easy to use. They also can be used to fish for all types and sizes of fish in almost all conditions.

A *baitcasting reel* is designed to be used with heavier rods, lines, and bait. Anglers use baitcasters when they are fishing for big bass and pike.

A *fly reel* is simpler than other types of reels. It looks kind of like a flattened spool. Fly reels are used only to store line between casts. They are not used to retrieve the lure. Instead, a fly fisher retrieves the lure, and lands the fish, by pulling directly on the line. This is used for small and medium fish.

This photo shows four types of reels.

fly reel — spincaster

baitcasting reel — spinning reel

SETTING THE DRAG

One of the most important jobs of the reel is to provide the right amount of resistance, or drag, when playing, or reeling in, a fish. The drag should be set so that a fish can pull some line out when it is fighting hard, but it should require the fish to use some force. All reels have a knob or lever to adjust drag. To set the drag

on a spinning or spincasting reel, hold the rod in one hand and pull on the line with the other. The rod should bend a little bit before the line starts coming off the reel.

TACKLING THE TACKLE BOX

Many people think that supplying and organizing your **tackle** box is one of the most enjoyable parts of fishing. Choose a tackle box that is the right size for your fishing style. It should have compartments in a variety of sizes to keep your tackle neat and organized so you can easily find whatever you want.

Here are some of the most important items in a well-stocked tackle box:

TACKLE BOX SUPPLIES

Hooks. Anglers lose a lot of hooks. They get snagged on weeds, rocks, and other underwater objects. Hooked fish sometimes cut the line with their teeth or break it by pulling hard on it. There will also be times that you will want to change from a larger to a smaller hook, or the other way around.

Bobbers. Bobbers are round or **oblong** floats that are attached to a line a certain distance above the bait. They float at the surface of the water, and their movement shows when a fish has taken the bait. Stock your tackle box with several bobbers of different sizes and shapes.

Sinkers. Sinkers are weights that drag your bait to the depth of the water where the fish are. Some sinkers are attached to the line with a hole, or eye. Others have a slit that can be pinched around the line. It is a good idea to have a variety of sinkers in different weights, shapes, and sizes.

Lures. **Lures** are artificial baits, and they come in a wide variety of shapes, sizes, materials, and colors. To get started, pick lures that are the right size for your rod and reel. If you really catch the fishing fever, you will probably make regular additions to your collection of lures.

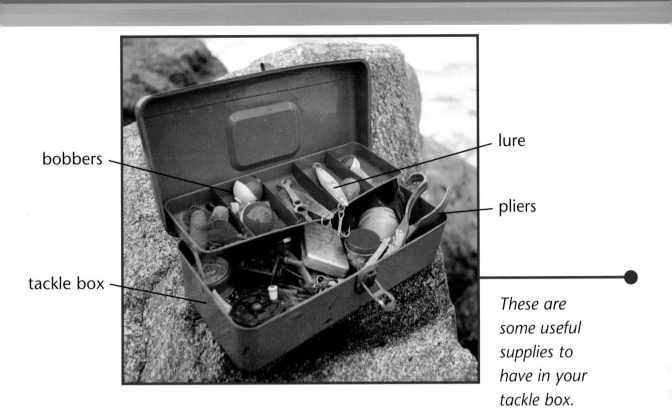

bobbers

lure

pliers

tackle box

These are some useful supplies to have in your tackle box.

Here are some other useful angling supplies:

OTHER ANGLING SUPPLIES

Needle-nosed pliers come in handy to bend hooks back into shape and to get hooks out of a fish's mouth.

Sunblock is important to protect your skin, especially your face and hands, from the sun's rays when outdoors.

A small *file* is useful for sharpening dull hooks.

A small *scale* and *ruler* will allow you to weigh and measure the fish you catch.

Polarized sunglasses are specially designed to filter out **glare** and allow you to see fish and other objects under the water. It is always important to use sunglasses to protect your eyes from bright sunlight.

CHOOSING YOUR BAIT

Choosing the right bait is a very important part of successful fishing. The first thing to consider when choosing bait is whether to use live or artificial bait.

LIVE BAIT

Live bait is the real food that fish eat, and fish are very willing to bite it. Live bait includes small fish such as minnows, chubs, dace, and shiners; worms; leeches; insects such as crickets, grasshoppers, mayflies, and various types of caterpillars; and crayfish.

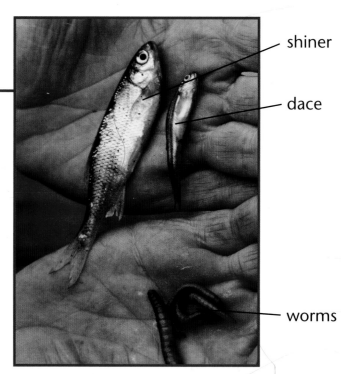

shiner

dace

worms

Many anglers use live bait, such as the bait in this picture, when they are learning how to fish. Other types of live bait include leeches, crayfish, and small frogs.

ARTIFICIAL BAIT

The many types of artificial bait, or **lures,** are designed to attract a fish's attention or to fool it into thinking a lure is food, or both. Some lures look a lot like live bait. Others are just brightly colored, or have flashy moving parts. Still others make noise as they move through the water.

DECIDING WHICH BAIT TO USE

A beginning angler might want to choose live bait over artificial because it is easier to catch fish with live bait. But artificial bait is more convenient to use. You do not have to worry about keeping it alive, as you do with live bait. You can keep it in your **tackle** box. As long as you do not lose it, you can use it over and over again.

In sunny, clear water, light-colored lures are usually better than darker ones. The opposite is true for dark, cloudy water. Another way to choose bait is to "match the hatch." This expression refers to the fact that fish eat **prey** that is available. When there are a lot of minnows available, they eat minnows. When certain kinds of insects hatch, such as mayflies, fish will be looking for mayflies. If you offer bait or lures that look like the type of prey the fish are eating, you will be more likely to catch fish.

LURES AND FLIES

Artificial bait includes spinners, plugs, jigs, soft plastics, spoons, and flies. Spinners have shiny metal blades that spin around as you retrieve them. Most plugs are made of plastic. They usually have two or more three-pronged hooks called treble hooks hanging from them. Jigs are simple lures made up of a hook with a lead weight molded around it. Soft plastics are rubbery and are designed to look and feel like live bait. Spoons are curved, blade-shaped lures that flash in the water. Most spoons are made of metal that is shiny on one side and brightly painted on the other. Most flies look like various types of insects. They are made by tying bits of hair, fur, or feathers onto a hook.

This picture shows a variety of lures.

SETTING UP YOUR RIG

Before you can start fishing, you will need to set up your **rig.** Each rig has the same basic parts, but may have a different kind of rod, reel, and bait setup. Here is how to set up a spinning rig with a sinker, a round bobber, and a hook baited with a worm.

ASSEMBLING THE ROD AND REEL

If your rod has two or three sections, you have to put it together. Hold the handle and gently slide the next section into the hole in the end of the handle section. Make sure the guides are lined up. Do the same with the third section, if there is one.

Now attach the reel. A spinning reel goes on the bottom side of the rod handle. Slide the reel's foot into the slot on the handle, called the reel seat. Slide the locking ring over the upper part of the reel foot and screw it on snugly.

TYING ON THE TACKLE

Pull some line from the reel and thread it through the circular guides on the rod. Use one of the angler's knots described on the next page to attach a hook to the end. To attach a sinker, slide the line into the slit on the sinker and use pliers to gently pinch the slit closed. Attach a bobber above the sinker by threading it through the loops at the top and bottom of the bobber.

There are several ways to attach a worm to a hook. You may hook the worm through the very end so that it moves freely in the water. Or you may slide the hook through the worm to hide the hook completely. You also may hook the worm several times to bunch it up.

BASIC ANGLER'S KNOTS

You can use these simple knots to attach a hook or **lure** to your line. When tying any knot, wet the line with water to make it slippery. Always trim the excess line with scissors close to the knot.

Trilene knot

1. Thread the line through the hook's eye twice to form a double loop.
2. Working upward from the loop, wrap the end of the line around the main line four or five times.
3. Thread the end of the line back through the double loop and pull tight.

Improved clinch knot

1. Pull about 6 inches (15 cm) of line through the eye of the hook.
2. Hold the end of the line against the main line and twist the hook around six times.
3. Thread the end of the line through the loop near the hook and then back through the loop above it.
4. Hold the end of the line and the main line and pull them snugly against the eye of the hook.

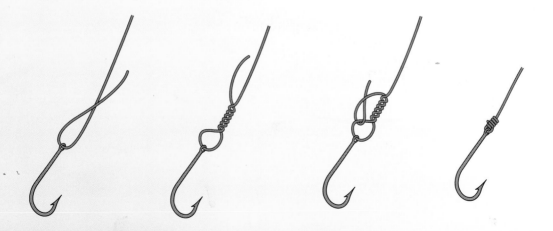

CASTING

The easiest way to cast is by simply throwing your line into the water. As you become a more experienced angler, you may want to learn various techniques for casting with different rods and reels. But as a beginner, you can start with learning two basic casts with a spinning reel.

A good way to remember the correct movements for casting is to picture a clock face. The important positions are 10 o'clock and 2 o'clock.

THE OVERHEAD CAST

Picture yourself standing directly in front of a giant clock, with your side to the clock face. Above your head is the 12 o'clock position.

1 Open the **bail** on the reel, and hook your index finger around the line.

2 Bring the rod back over your shoulder to point to where the 2 would be on the clock (if you are right-handed) or where the 10 would be on the clock (if you are left-handed). Look at the photo on the left for a demonstration of how to do this.

3 Pitch the rod forward smoothly. When your rod gets to about the 10 o'clock position (for right-handers) or the 2 o'clock position (for left-handers), remove your index finger from the line. See photo on the right for an example.

THE SIDEARM CAST

Picture yourself standing in the middle of a clock face, with your casting arm at 12 o'clock. Your head would be pointing to the 3 on the clock.

1 Open the bail on the reel, and hook your index finger around the line.

2 Bring the rod back behind you to about the 2 o'clock position if you are right-handed or the 10 o'clock position if you are left-handed.

3 Pitch the rod forward smoothly. When your rod gets to about the 10 o'clock position (for right-handers) or the 2 o'clock position (for left-handers), remove your index finger from the line.

FLY CASTING

Fly casting uses a special type of rod, reel, line, and lures called flies. The angler retrieves the fly in a technique called stripping, in which he or she pulls directly on the line with the fingers. Fish often strike during stripping.

FINDING FISH

The two most important keys to successful fishing are knowing where the fish are and what the fish want. To figure out these things, experienced anglers look at a number of conditions such as weather, season, water temperature, the kind of fish they are fishing for, and the natural food available to the fish.

This smallmouth bass might be seeking other fish to feed on around this underwater rock structure.

One of the first things to know about fish is that they like **structures.** A structure is any type of underwater object that provides a good place for fish to hide and eat. A structure could be the hull of a sunken boat; a pile of logs, dead trees, or rocks; a weed bed; a dock or pier; or anything else that makes fish feel safe and secure. If you can find a structure, you will probably find fish.

MORE WAYS TO FIND FISH

Another way to find fish is to watch for signs of the fish themselves. Ripples on the surface of the water, a large splash, or a disturbance of smaller fish, or bait fish, can all be signs that a big fish is active nearby. Also pay attention to fish-eating water birds, such as herons, egrets, pelicans, and terns. Such birds often gather to feed on schools, or groups, of bait fish. Bigger fish do the same thing. So follow the birds to the bait fish and you might catch some fish.

POPULAR FRESHWATER SPORT FISH

	Name	Average length or weight	What is special about this fish?
	Northern pike	2 to 10 pounds (0.9–4.5 kg)	fierce **predator,** great fighter
	Muskellunge, also known as muskie	2 to 4 feet (0.6–1.2 m)	largest pike
	Largemouth bass	1 to 4 pounds (0.5–1.8 kg)	most popular freshwater game fish, known for spectacular leaps when hooked
	Yellow perch	5–12 in. (13–30 cm)	easy to catch
	Bluegill	less than 10 inches (25 cm)	beautifully colored
	Rainbow trout	1 to 3 pounds (0.5–1.4 kg)	much larger in lakes; known for spectacular leaps when hooked
	Walleye	12 to 36 inches (30.5–91 cm)	white tip on bottom of tail, light-reflecting eyes
	Channel catfish	2 to 3 pounds (0.9–1.4 kg)	no scales, poisonous spine on back fin

PLAYING AND LANDING FISH

The first step in catching a fish is getting a bite. You will know when you have a bite if you sense something alive on the end of your rod. Your rod tip might jerk lightly a few times. It may slowly bend with a kind of heavy feeling. Sometimes fish strike, or bite aggressively and hard. After a strike, the fish may "smoke" and the line may start spinning off the reel as the fish tries to swim away quickly.

SETTING THE HOOK AND PLAYING THE FISH

Now is the time to act fast and set the hook. You do this by quickly snapping up the tip of the rod to drive the hook into the fish's lip. Once you know the fish is hooked, keep steady pressure on the line as you reel in. If you let the line go limp, you give the fish a chance to spit out the hook or shake it out of its mouth. Raise the rod tip up to pull the fish toward you. Then lower it and reel only when there is slack in the line. If the fish starts swimming away, let it run. When it stops, once again pull the fish toward you, drop the rod tip, and reel in the slack. Repeat these actions until the fish is close to the boat.

Use extra caution when you are fishing from slippery surfaces, such as rocks, that are near water.

LANDING THE FISH

Small fish can be **landed** by simply lifting them into the boat. You might need help to land a larger fish. Hold the rod upright and keep the fish close to the boat and near the surface. A friend can then scoop the fish up in a net to avoid harming it. Fish such as bass, which do not have true teeth, can be landed by grabbing the bottom jaw with the thumb inside the mouth and the rest of the fingers cupping the **gill plate**.

Always make sure your hand is wet when you pick up a fish to avoid removing the fish's protective layer of slime. Also, fins and gill plates can be sharp, so use caution.

CATCH AND RELEASE

Many fishers practice catch-and-release angling. To make sure the fish is returned to the water unharmed, remember these points:

- Handle the fish as little as possible. Remove the hook quickly and gently. If the hook is too deeply embedded in the fish's mouth, cut the line and leave the hook in. The hook will eventually dissolve.

- If you want to take a picture, have the camera ready before you take the fish from the water.

- Do not release the fish until it has recovered from being caught. Swish it gently back and forth under the water. The fish is ready to be released when its gill movements are strong and regular and when it can stay upright in the water.

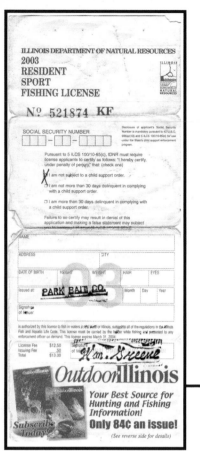

This is what a typical fishing license looks like.

Each state has rules controlling where, when, and how people may fish. The rules vary from state to state. They may also vary within a state in different bodies of water. It is important to know the rules of fishing in your location. The department of natural resources in every state publishes a booklet that explains all the fishing rules for that state.

In most cases, you will need to have a fishing license. Licenses are usually available for different periods, such as a one-day license, one-week license, or a one-year license. You may buy a fishing license at bait shops, sporting goods stores, and fishing resorts. You must have the license with you whenever you are fishing in public waters.

KEEPING FISH HEALTHY

Many rules are intended to keep the fish populations healthy. Most states have **regulations** about when fishing is allowed. For instance, most states do not allow fishing for certain **species** of fish when they are **spawning.** Most fish are active and easy to catch during spawning. If they are caught before they have a chance to lay their eggs, a whole generation of new fish is lost. These rules protect the fish and allow them to **reproduce.**

Do not fish in areas with signs like this one posted.

Other rules restrict the number and size of fish each angler can keep. For example, you may be allowed to take home only two, six, ten, or twenty of certain types of fish. Or you may have to release any fish that is smaller than a certain size limit. Another kind of size limit is called a slot limit. A slot limit says that you cannot keep any fish of a certain species that falls within a certain size range. For example, in some places, anglers are not allowed to keep any walleyes that are between 20 inches (51 centimeters) and 24 inches (61 centimeters) long. Walleyes of this size usually produce the most offspring.

Many anglers begin fishing at a very young age.

FISHING SAFETY

Fishing is a fun, exciting sport. Following a few simple rules makes it a safe one, too.

- Always wear a life preserver when fishing.

- Be careful when handling hooks. They are sharp.

- Look around and behind you before casting to make sure you do not snag anyone.

- Use care when handling fish. Some have sharp teeth, fins, and gill covers that can cause bad cuts.

- Protect your eyes and face from the sun and **glare** from the water by wearing a hat and sunglasses. Do not forget to use sunscreen, too.

It is a great feeling to be able to go out into nature and get your own food. Fish are also nutritious and delicious. They are low in fat and high in protein. They also contain substances called fatty acids, which help keep your **nervous system** healthy.

IS EATING FISH HARMFUL?

Some caution is needed when eating fish. Substances such as mercury and other chemicals sometimes get into the bodies of fish in water. These pollutants then pass into people's bodies when they eat the fish. As a result, some health experts suggest that people limit the amount of fish they eat. They also recommend that people avoid eating the fattiest parts of fish, such as the belly and the meat along the back and at the sides.

Anglers must learn how to clean and prepare a fish for cooking.

Many anglers enjoy cooking the fish they catch over an open fire.

Broiling, sauteing, deep-frying, pan frying, grilling, smoking, and baking are some of the most popular ways to prepare fish. Fish is also delicious in stir-fries and soups.

PAN-FRIED FISH COATING

Pan frying is a popular way to prepare fish, and most anglers have their own favorite recipes for fish coating, which is also known as breading. Here is a recipe that you can try yourself.

1/2 cup (110 grams) cornmeal
1 cup (230 grams) flour
1 teaspoon salt
1/2 teaspoon pepper
2 teaspoon paprika
1 teaspoon garlic powder
1 teaspoon poultry seasoning or other herb mixture
Four fish fillets about an inch (2.5 centimeters) thick
Oil for frying

Mix the first seven ingredients on a piece of wax paper. One at a time, place a fish fillet in the coating mixture. Turn and pat each fillet so that they are well coated.

Pour oil into a steep sided frying pan to a depth of about half an inch (1.3 centimeters). Have an adult heat the oil on medium heat until it is hot. The oil is at the right temperature when a little bit of coating mixture sizzles when dropped in the oil.

Have an adult place the fish in the oil. Cook the fillets about six minutes on each side. Adjust the cooking time for larger or smaller fillets.

Drain the fillets on paper towels before serving.

COMPETITIONS

You might not think of fishing as a competitive sport, but it is. Every year there are hundreds of fishing tournaments, including **professional** tournaments for big-money prizes. Tournaments for **amateurs** are sponsored by fishing clubs and other organizations. Some amateur tournaments are just for fun. Others provide a way for serious fishers to work their way up to professional tournaments.

The most popular kind of tournaments are bass-fishing tournaments. Walleye tournaments are also popular. The winner is usually the angler who catches the most fish according to weight in a certain amount of time. For example, an angler who catches two fish that weigh a total of 8 pounds (3.6 kg) would beat an angler who catches three fish whose combined weight is 7 pounds (3.2 kg).

This 77-pound (35-kg) amberjack fish was caught at a tournament in Georgia in 1996.

FISHING DERBY FOR KIDS

The largest fishing program for kids is the Kids All-American Fishing Derby. The program consists of about 1,800 separate competitions that happen nationwide every year from April to October. Kids from the ages of 5 to 16 fish in different contests. For example, the Big Fish Contest allows the boy or girl who catches the biggest fish in their local derby to enter a drawing for a chance to win prizes.

WORLD-RECORD FRESHWATER FISH

Type of fish	Weight	Place caught	Year
Bluegill	4 pounds 12 ounces (2.2 kg)	Ketona Lake, Alabama	1950
Brook trout	14 pounds 8 ounces (6.6 kg)	Nipigon River, Ontario	1916
Chinook salmon	97 pounds 4 ounces (44 kg)	Kenai River, Alaska	1985
Cutthroat trout	41 pounds 0 ounces (18.6 kg)	Pyramid Lake, Nevada	1925
Flathead catfish	123 pounds 0 ounces (55.8 kg)	Elk City Reservoir, Kansas	1998
Largemouth bass	22 pounds 4 ounces (10.1 kg)	Montgomery Lake, Georgia	1932
Muskellunge	67 pounds 8 ounces (30.6 kg)	Hayward, Wisconsin	1949
Northern pike	55 pounds 1 ounce (25 kg)	Lake of Grefeern, Germany	1986
Rainbow trout	42 pounds 2 ounces (19.1 kg)	Bell Island, Alaska	1970
Smallmouth bass	10 pounds 14 ounces (4.9 kg)	Dale Hollow Reservoir, Tennessee	1969
Walleye	25 pounds 0 ounces (11.3 kg)	Old Hickory Lake, Tennessee	1960
White crappie	5 pounds 3 ounces (2.4 kilograms)	Enid Dam, Mississippi	1957
Yellow perch	4 pounds 3 ounces (1.9 kilograms)	Delaware River, New Jersey	1865

Anywhere there is a body of water, you will probably find anglers. With the widespread availability of fishing **tackle,** freshwater sport fishing is similar throughout the world. What is different are the types of fish anglers catch.

Sport anglers in India cast their lines into the rivers hoping to catch the majestic golden mahseer. This fish regularly grows up to 70 pounds (31.8 kg) and can reach 125 pounds (56.7 kg).

The Amazon River has an incredible number of amazing sport fish. One of the most popular and beautiful is the peacock bass. These fish can grow to well over 20 pounds (9.1 kilograms). Anglers catch them in quiet **lagoons** that are attached to the river. Peacock bass are not true bass, such as the largemouth and smallmouth bass of North America. Instead, they are part of a family of tropical freshwater fish called cichlids.

Mahseer can grow to be very large. They have lips that are good for eating things from the bottoms of lakes and rivers.

OTHER AMAZON FISH

Other giant Amazon fish are the *arapaima* and the *payara.* The *arapaima* has to breathe air at the surface. The *payara* is a fearsome **predator** with long, razor-sharp teeth in its lower jaw. This fish's strength and fighting ability provide a thrilling experience for anglers.

The *taimen* is a large fish of eastern Asia. These fish are believed to be a more ancient form of the salmon and trout of North America. In the rivers of Siberia, *taimen* can reach huge sizes. The largest recorded *taimen* weighed in at almost 250 pounds (113.4 kg).

In Asia and tropical Africa, one of the most popular game fish is the hard-fighting snakehead. These fish have tasty flesh and grow up to three feet (one meter) in length.

TALE OF A TAIMEN

According to a Mongolian folktale, a group of lost and starving tribesmen found a giant *taimen* frozen in the ice. They survived all winter long by cutting pieces of flesh from the fish. When the ice began to melt in the spring, the tribesmen were astonished to see the great fish wiggle free from the ice and swim away!

These snakehead fish were photographed using their fins to move along the ground. Snakehead fish have been found in the United States and could threaten local fish populations.

UNWELCOME SETTLERS

The snakehead made news in the United States in 2002 when two adult snakeheads and about 100 of their young were discovered in a Maryland lake. Wildlife officials determined that the two adult fish came from an Asian food market. Snakeheads also have been found in lakes and ponds in several states. Wildlife officials fear that if the population of these fish-gobbling predators grows, it may threaten many **species** of **native** fish.

GLOSSARY

amateur	person who does something for enjoyment rather than for money
archaeologist	scientist who learns about ancient people by studying their tools, buildings, and utensils
bail	part of a reel that either allows or prevents line coming off the spool
fiberglass	glass in the form of very fine threads. Fiberglass is blended with plastic to make fishing rods.
gill plate	flap of bone that covers a fish's gill
glare	harsh, brilliant light
graphite	soft, black mineral that is used to make fishing rods
lagoon	small, shallow pond connected to a larger body of water
land	to catch a fish
lure	artificial bait used for catching fish
native	living or growing in nature in a particular area or region
nervous system	bodily system that sends nerve impulses to organs that make actions. In humans, the nervous system includes the brain, spinal cord, and nerves.
oblong	longer in one direction than the other
predator	animal that kills and eats other animals in order to live
prey	animal that is hunted or killed by other animals for food
professional	person that does something for money rather than just for enjoyment
regulation	rule that explains the way something should be done
reproduce	produce new individuals, or offspring, of the same kind
retrieve	to reel in a lure
rig	rod, reel, and bait or lure that are set up and used for angling
spawn	to produce new young, sometimes by laying and fertilizing eggs
species	category of living, related things that are able to produce offspring
structure	any type of underwater object that provides a good place for fish to hide and eat
synthetic	not existing naturally; human-made
tackle	all the equipment used for angling

MORE BOOKS TO READ

Drinkard, G. Lawson. *Fishing in a Brook: Angling Activities for Kids.* Layton, Ut.: Gibbs Smith, 2000.

Maas, Dave. *Kids Gone Fishin'.* Chanhassen, Minn.: Creative Publishing International, 2001.

Morey, Shaun. *Kids' Incredible Fishing Stories.* New York: Workman, 1999.

Smith, Tim. *Buck Wilder's Small Fry Fishing Guide: A Complete Introduction to the World of Fishing for Small Fry of All Ages.* Williamsburg, Mich.: Alexander & Smith, 2003.

TAKING IT FURTHER

American Sportfishing Association
225 Reinekers Lane
Suite 420
Alexandria, VA 22314
info@asafishing.org

Hooked on Fishing International
Kids All-American Fishing Derby
P.O. Box 660
Ketchum, OK 74349
info@kids-fishing.com

National Fish and
Wildlife Foundation
1120 Connecticut Ave., NW
Suite 900
Washington, D.C. 20036

Recreational Boating and
Fishing Foundation
601 N. Fairfax St., Suite 140
Alexandria, VA 22314

INDEX

Africa 6, 29
Amazon River 28
angling, the sport of 5, 7
angling supplies 10–11
Asia 29

bail 8
bait 12–13
    artificial bait 10, 12,
      13
    live bait 12, 13, 14
    lures 10, 11, 12, 13
baitcasting reels 9
bite, getting a 4, 20
bobbers 10, 11, 14
books on fishing 6, 31

casting 16–17, 23
    fly casting 17
    overhead cast 16
    sidearm cast 17
catch-and-release
  angling 21
China 6
competitions 26
cooking and eating fish
  24–5
cranks 8

drag 9

Egypt, ancient 6
electronic devices 7

fiberglass rods 7, 8
fish
    around the world 28–9
    finding 18
    freshwater sport fish
      19, 27
    handling 21, 23
    world records 27
fishing expressions 7
flies 13, 17
floats 10

fly casting 17
fly reels 9

graphite rods 8
Greece, ancient 6

history of fishing 6–7
hooking the fish 4, 20
hooks 6, 10, 11, 13, 23
    attaching 14
    removing 21
    worms, attaching 14

India 28

jigs 13

Kids All-American Fishing
  Derby 26
knots 15
    improved clinch knot
      15
    trilene knot 15

landing the fish 8, 21
licenses 22
lures 10, 11, 12, 13
    retrieving 8, 9

pain, causing 5
playing the fish 20
pliers 11, 14
plugs 13
popularity of angling 7

reel seat 8, 14
reeling in the catch 4
reels 7, 8–9
    attaching to the rod
      14
    baitcasting reels 9
    crank 8
    fly reels 9
    setting the drag 9
    spincasters 8, 9

spinning reels 7, 8, 9,
  14
spool 8
rig 8
    setting up 14–15
    see also bait; reels;
      rods
rods 7, 8
    assembling 14
    materials 8
rules 22–3

safety 11, 20, 23
satellite technology 7
sinkers 10, 14
slot limits 23
snakehead fish 29
soft plastics 13
spawning 22
spearing fish 6
spincasters 8, 9
spinners 13, 13
spinning reels 8, 9, 14
spools 8
spoons 13
sun safety 11, 23

tackle box 10–11
tournaments 26

weighing and measuring
  the fish 11
world records 27

young anglers 26